BRIAN JOHNSTON

A Greater Sense of God

A Divine Invitation to Intimacy

HAYES PRESS Christian Publisher

First published by Hayes Press 2021

Copyright © 2021 by Brian Johnston

All rights reserved. No part of this publication may be reproduced, stored or transmitted in any form or by any means, electronic, mechanical, photocopying, recording, scanning, or otherwise without written permission from the publisher. It is illegal to copy this book, post it to a website, or distribute it by any other means without permission.

Brian Johnston asserts the moral right to be identified as the author of this work.

Brian Johnston has no responsibility for the persistence or accuracy of URLs for external or third-party Internet Websites referred to in this publication and does not guarantee that any content on such Websites is, or will remain, accurate or appropriate.

Unless otherwise stated, scripture quotations are taken from the (NASB®) New American Standard Bible®, Copyright © 1960, 1971, 1977, 1995, 2020 by The Lockman Foundation. Used by permission. All rights reserved. www.lockman.org.

Scripture quotations marked (NIV) are taken from the Holy Bible, New International Version®, NIV®. Copyright © 1973, 1978, 1984, 2011 by Biblica, Inc.™ Used by permission of Zondervan. All rights reserved worldwide. www.zondervan.comThe "NIV" and "New International Version" are trademarks registered in the United States Patent and Trademark Office by Biblica, Inc.™

First edition

This book was professionally typeset on Reedsy. Find out more at reedsy.com

Contents

Foreword		iv
1	A Vivid Experience	1
2	A Mobile Throne	7
3	A Declining Culture	14
4	A Close Encounter	21
5	Standing Firm	27
6	Becoming Sanctified	34
7	A Compassionate King	40
8	Living Your Best Life	46
9	Outwards from the Innermost	53
10	From Eternity to Eternity	60
11	A Worthy Distinction	66
12	Responding to Revelation	72
ABOUT THE AUTHOR		79
MORE BOOKS BY BRIAN JOHNSTON		80
ABOUT THE PUBLISHER		84

Foreword

It was a Tuesday morning and I'd a meeting with a team of scientists from the United States that morning. The date was the 28th of January, 1986. It's etched in my memory because it was the date of the Space Shuttle Challenger disaster. To this day, I distinctly recall how before our meeting with the U.S. scientists began that morning, my immediate superior reached out to the team leader opposite and offered condolences for the loss of the seven astronauts who in exiting gravity had entered eternity.

It had been watched live by millions, for only 73 secs after lift-off from Cape Canaveral, the Space Shuttle had exploded. President Reagan that day gave quite a speech. He talked of "space as the last frontier." And of how "pioneers have always given their lives on the frontier." He later paraphrased a poem by an Air Force volunteer, saying that they "slipped the surly bonds of earth ... and touched the face of God."[1]

"Touching God's face" - that's an extremely evocative expression. It suggests intimacy, as with someone we know well. We come close to God through prayer. In the language of the Bible, we

---

[1] High Flight by John Gillespie Mageee https://nationalpoetryday.co.uk/poem/high-flight/

often find expressions such as "seeking God's face." It's a way of describing prayer. And, even more expressive than that, we occasionally come across the still more striking phrase: "the softening of his face", that is literally, the softening of God's face (e.g. Exodus 32:11; 1 Kings 13:6; 2 Kings 13:4; Malachi 1:9). That, in turn, may suggest soothing, possibly by touching, and it's an idiom used of a particular type of prayer known as intercessory prayer. We're back to the implied intimacy of touching the face of God. One of the most amazing revelations about God in the Bible is that he wants you and me to become intimate with him - and the goal of this book is simply to help that become a reality.

1

A Vivid Experience

The Bible is full of the records of people who experienced God slipping into their life from another dimension and changing their lives for ever. I've known times when extraordinary things have happened and been equally sure my part was only to contribute the ordinary while God had slipped in and supplied the extra. The results have been lasting. The greatest example that all Christian believers share is their conversion experience when they encountered God through his Word, the Bible. Though logical and philosophical arguments for the existence of God are compelling – at least as compelling as any argument of that type can be – how much more satisfying when we have a concrete or even sensory experience of God, as in sensing him breaking through into the everyday humdrum of our lives and changing them permanently.

God reveals himself to us that we may know him. He wants us to have a relationship with him. The Good News of the Christian message is news of a new deal (God calls it a new covenant, something like a contract): God says it's not any matter of external religion, but he'll write his laws on our hearts. He says guilt will not haunt us, for he totally reassures us that he'll 'no more' remember our sins. Most importantly of all, he says we'll know him (Hebrews 8:10-12). Christian author Jim Packer in his classic book *Knowing God*, wrote: "Not many of us, I think, would ever naturally say that we have known God. The words imply a definiteness and matter-of-factness of experience to which most of us, if we are honest, have to admit that we are still strangers ... with most of us experience of God has never become so vivid as that."[2] With Ezekiel, his experience of God was about to become very vivid. We'll let the Bible prophet take up his own story ...

> *"... while I was by the river Chebar among the exiles, the heavens were opened and I saw visions of God. (On the fifth of the month in the fifth year of King Jehoiachin's exile, the word of the Lord came expressly to Ezekiel the priest, son of Buzi, in the land of the Chaldeans by the river Chebar; and there the hand of the Lord came upon him"* (Ezekiel 1:1-3).

Forgive me if I interrupt the account here; I simply want to explain the prophet Eziekiel's circumstances. Clearly, he's not anywhere in the land of Israel at this point, but in the land of the Chaldeans. He's told us that he's among the exiles. God's ancient people, Israel, had been extremely disloyal to the God who'd treated them well. After many warnings and appeals, God did as he had warned and permitted them to be taken captive, transported to Babylon. And Ezekiel finds himself

---

[2] Knowing God, J.I. Packer, p.21, Hodder Christian Paperbacks edition, 1973

among them, although I think we can assume his behaviour hadn't been like that of his compatriots. But God had a purpose in him being among the exiles in a foreign land. We'll let him continue to share his experience with us ...

> *"As I looked, behold, a high wind was coming from the north, a great cloud with fire flashing intermittently and a bright light around it, and in its midst something like gleaming metal in the midst of the fire ... there was something resembling a throne, like lapis lazuli in appearance; and on that which resembled a throne, high up, was a figure with the appearance of a man. Then I noticed from the appearance of His waist and upward something like gleaming metal that looked like fire all around within it, and from the appearance of His waist and downward I saw something like fire; and there was a radiance around Him. Like the appearance of the rainbow in the clouds on a rainy day, so was the appearance of the surrounding radiance. Such was the appearance of the likeness of the glory of the Lord. And when I saw it, I fell on my face and heard a voice speaking"* (Ezekiel 1:4,26-28).

I'm sure that was the day when God became much more real to Ezekiel, for it must have been an unforgettable experience. Vivid, certainly. A storm can be a captivating sight on its own, but in this case it was simply the awesome vehicle through which God graphically displayed the splendour of his being to his prophet. Why were certain prophets such as Ezekiel and Isaiah privileged to have such experiences of God? One reason, for sure, is that God had very difficult ministries for them to fulfil. When their audiences would prove stubbornly unresponsive, it must have been so tempting for them to want to give up or to wonder what was the point. There would be many times when they'd need to fall back on the memory of that very vivid encounter with God.

Such a glimpse of the splendour of God was also necessary to make Ezekiel's ministry totally authentic. This is because the major theme of his message to his people was about their need to know God. How do we know this? It's simply because on so many, many occasions he'd have to announce to the people, speaking on God's behalf, and saying to them: *"that you may know that I am the LORD."* Try counting how many times these words are recorded in the Bible book that bears Ezekiel's name. You'll find the words *"that you may know that I am the LORD"* more than sixty times. And what that has to show – and this is so important – is that this is the great need of the Lord's people at any time. God's people's great need is to know God in all his total otherness as revealed in Scripture, and to become like him in all his communicable attributes.

There would appear to be four main ways in which God makes himself known through Ezekiel. He reveals his splendour, his transcendence, his holiness and his judgments. And this disclosure was to a people who were ruined; whose own existence was fleeting; whose sinfulness was scarcely imaginable; and who deserved only judgement from God. It's here we find stark contrasts of his splendour over against human ruin; of divine transcendence over against human transitoriness; of his holiness over against human sinfulness; but also of his mercy for his own name's sake over against the judgement rebellious humans truly deserve. Yes, the book of Ezekiel is a picture painted in strongly contrasting colours.

And so we must begin our studies where God began with his prophet Ezekiel – with a dazzling display of his majestic splendour. God makes himself known to us as a God who is glorious in holiness. And basically, his holiness is his otherness. God is like no other. There is no-one like the LORD. He alone is without beginning. He is absolutely sovereign. He is the immutable God, that is, the unchanging God. God repeatedly declares himself to us in these categories. There is no glory like the glory of the LORD. What the prophet saw was clearly beyond what words could adequately convey. There's a sense that he's struggling to express himself here. He's trying to describe something resembling the appearance of the likeness of the glory of the LORD. It's really too wonderful for words. We're talking about knowing God in these studies; Moses was someone who once said to God: *"let me know ... You, ... show me Your glory"* (Exodus 33:13-18). God's response to that request by Moses is recorded in Exodus chapter 34:

> *"Then the Lord passed by in front of him and proclaimed, 'The Lord, the Lord God, compassionate and merciful, slow to anger, and abounding in faithfulness and truth; who keeps faithfulness for thousands, who forgives wrongdoing, violation of His Law, and sin; yet He will by no means leave the guilty unpunished, inflicting the punishment of fathers on the children and on the grandchildren to the third and fourth generations.' And Moses hurried to bow low toward the ground and worship"* (Exodus 34:6-8).

And well might he. At the very core of that self-revelation of God is the word (*hesed*, faithful love) that may be translated as 'goodness' but is properly captured by the thought of supreme generosity. Right away, we can see the most fundamental difference between God and ourselves. God is 'other-centred' whereas sin has made us all to be self-centred, admittedly some more so than others, apparently. When God shared this cluster of his own moral perfections, he spoke of himself as 'abundant in goodness and truth.' This goodness or lovingkindness is the quality of generosity[3]: giving to others consistently beyond what the recipients deserve (this is grace). This focal point of God's moral perfection is the quality of wishing others should have what they need to make them happy.

Now, I promise you we're going to wrap up this chapter with a truth involved in coming to really know God that's almost too wonderful to absorb. And it's this: that God has chosen to make his happiness to be dependent on ours. As Packer said,[4] "through setting His love on men God has voluntarily bound up His own final happiness with theirs." On that, we need to meditate and pray and praise until the fact becomes part of our true knowledge of the God of majestic spendour and transcendent glory.

---

[3] Knowing God, p.180

[4] Knowing God, p.138

2

A Mobile Throne

You've most probably heard the saying: 'If God seems far away, guess who's moved?' The suggestion being made is that periods in our personal life when God seems distant are down to us have drifted spiritually. But in this study, we're going to track a time when it was definitely God who moved.

I'm generally content with anything second-hand, but second-hand knowledge of God is the route to spiritual impoverishment. And we're going to see that demonstrated among the people of God in Ezekiel's day. As Packer says: "We must learn to measure ourselves, not by our knowledge about God, not by our gifts and responsibilities in the church, but by how we pray and what goes on in our hearts. Many of us, I suspect, have no idea how impoverished we are on this level. Let us ask the Lord to show us."[5] Perhaps, he can use the prophet Ezekiel and what we find in the Bible Book that bears his name. His book, as we've already seen, is one that opens with a vision that was

---

[5] Knowing God, J.I. Packer, p.30, Hodder Christian Paperbacks edition, 1973

given to him – a vision of the splendour of the God of glory:

"Like the appearance of the rainbow in the clouds on a rainy day, so was the appearance of the surrounding radiance. Such was the appearance of the likeness of the glory of the Lord. And when I saw it, I fell on my face and heard a voice speaking" (Ezekiel 1:28).

That's the splendour of God, I'm sure you'll agree. But this is a book of very vivid contrasts. Alongside the splendour of God, we're brought face to face with the total ruination of God's people. On the one hand, the book presents God as glorious and sovereign. For example, we read of Egypt being given to Babylon by God as wages for their defeat of Tyre. But, on the other hand, it presents the people of God as ruined and defeated. Ruined by their lack of knowledge of God - or even the lack of any desire on their part to have it. For they had rebelled against it:

"Then He said to me, 'Son of man, I am sending you to the sons of Israel, to a rebellious people who have rebelled against Me ... and you shall say to them, "This is what the Lord God says: As for them, whether they listen or not—for they are a rebellious house—they will know that a prophet has been among them" ... But you shall speak My words to them whether they listen or not, for they are rebellious'" (Ezekiel 2:3-7).

And so it was that to these people, Ezekiel was called to bring God's message - to a people who'd constantly rebelled against God. They're repeatedly described as a rebellious house "Then

He said to me, *"Son of man, go to the house of Israel and speak with My words to them ... yet the house of Israel will not be willing to listen to you, since they are not willing to listen to Me"* (Ezekiel 3:4-7). As Ezekiel begins to bring God's message to this people, he charts for us the movement of the glory of the LORD as he journals his experience of God:

> *"Go to the exiles, to the sons of your people, and speak to them and tell them, whether they listen or not, 'This is what the Lord God says.'" Then the Spirit lifted me up, and I heard a great rumbling sound behind me: "Blessed be the glory of the Lord from His place!"* (Ezekiel 3:11,12).

> *"And He ... brought me in the visions of God to Jerusalem, to the entrance of the north gate of the inner courtyard, where the seat of the idol of jealousy, which provokes to jealousy, was located. And behold, the glory of the God of Israel was there, like the appearance which I saw in the plain"* (Ezekiel 8:3,4).

This is God giving his prophet an altogether different vision now: a glimpse of the ruined state of those whose high calling had been to serve the true and living God of glory:

> *"Then He brought me into the inner courtyard of the Lord's house. And behold, at the entrance to the temple of the Lord, between the porch and the altar, were about twenty-five men with their backs to the temple of the Lord while their faces were toward the east; and they were prostrating themselves eastward toward the sun"* (Ezekiel 8:16).

As a consequence of this, we notice – with Ezekiel - the gradual slow movement of God's glory away from the Jerusalem Temple: *"Then the glory of the God of Israel ascended from the cherub on which it had been, to the threshold of the temple"* (Ezekiel 9:3). It's a gradual withdrawal. God is reluctant to leave, but his people leave him no choice, having rebelled in refusing to know him and his ways:

> *"Then the glory of the Lord departed from the threshold of the temple and stood over the cherubim. When the cherubim departed, they lifted their wings and rose up from the ground in my sight with the wheels beside them; and they stood still at the entrance of the east gate of the Lord's house, and the glory of the God of Israel hovered over them"* (Ezekiel 10:18,19).

Little by little, stage by stage, God's glorious presence is retreating from its former residence in the Temple, and God sounds a warning to his persistently rebellious people:

> *"You will fall by the sword. I will judge you to the border of Israel; so you shall know that I am the Lord. This city will not be a pot for you, nor will you be meat in the midst of it; I will judge you to the border of Israel. So you will know that I am the Lord; for you have not walked in My statutes, nor have you executed My ordinances, but you have acted in accordance with the ordinances of the nations around you"* (Ezekiel 11:10-12).

Notice the repetition of the root cause behind God's departure. They'd lost the knowledge of God and needed to learn it again through this bitter experience. Knowledge of God is the basis of eternal life, as the Apostle John notes Jesus saying in the New Testament, *"Now this is eternal life: that they may know you, the only true God, and Jesus Christ, whom you have sent"* (John 17:3). Not only is the knowledge of God the basis of eternal life, but continued growth in the knowledge of God is the essence of that life.

Although the promise and revelation about eternal life had to await the coming of Christ in the New Testament, it's still true that the outstanding deficit with God's Old Testament people, as recorded in the Book of Ezekiel, was their lack of the knowledge of God. More than sixty times, the prophet Ezekiel talks about people – either God's own people or their neighbours – needing to come to know God. It was their greatest need. And it's the greatest need of God's people at any time, even when we – who may claim to be God's people - haven't fallen down as far as Israel or Judah had at that time. The transportation of God's people happened in stages or waves. Those left behind in Jerusalem at this stage were boasting that they still possessed the land (with its Temple). Ezekiel is told: *"... your fellow exiles ... are those to whom the inhabitants of Jerusalem have said, 'Keep far from the Lord; this land has been given to us as a possession'"* (Ezekiel 11:15).

We should say that Ezekiel preached to God's people in the sixth century BC for some 22 years during their Babylonian captivity. What was it that had brought God's people to ruin? They'd taken their God for granted. They'd assumed that God's covenant with their forefathers was irrevocable. They'd presumed the (continuous) ownership of the land was permanent. They thought that some of them would remain immune to any foreign captivity as long as God or at least his temple was standing in Jerusalem. As Packer says: "We must learn to measure ourselves, not by our knowledge about God, not by our gifts and responsibilities in the church, but by how we pray and what goes on in our hearts."[6]

As for Israel, God would bring them back and restore them to their land but first he'd have to interrupt their continuous enjoyment of it because of their rebellious refusal to have him in their knowledge. God would first abandon his city entirely. Ezekiel saw it happening quite graphically: *"Then ... the glory of the Lord went up from the midst of the city and stood over the mountain which is east of the city"* (Ezekiel 11:22,23). In the western world today, God's Word, generally speaking, is no longer respected. It's because people have turned away from desiring to know God. The Apostle Paul says:

> *"For even though they knew God, they did not honor Him as God or give thanks, but they became futile in their reasonings, and their senseless hearts were darkened. Claiming to be wise, they became fools, and they exchanged the glory of the incorruptible God for an image in the form of corruptible mankind* [man became the measure of all things], *of birds, four-footed animals, and crawling creatures. Therefore God gave them up ..."* (Romans 1:21-24).

... to impurity, degrading passions, indecent acts and the

---

[6] Knowing God, J.I. Packer, p.30, Hodder Christian Paperbacks edition, 1973

exchanging of natural functions for that which is unnatural. To rebel against the knowledge of God brings the ruin of any human society. We're slow to learn the lessons of history.

Recent analyses of global Christianity show that Christianity isn't shrinking, but it is shifting. It's shifting its centre of gravity from the great land masses of North America and Europe in 1900 to sub-Saharan Africa and East Asia by the time the year 2020 had arrived. God, certainly in terms of his evident working, has been moving out of western society as it increasingly refuses to know him, and becomes more and more secular. And in the writing of constitutions and legislation increasingly hostile to God and the Bible, we have in our time – just like Ezekiel – a perception of God moving further and further away.

3

A Declining Culture

Ezekiel was Jeremiah's contemporary. Although born into a priestly family, Ezekiel was denied temple service just when he should have been graduating into a full role in it. For in 597 B.C., he, together with the royalty, the nobles, and many of the leading priests and craftsmen, was transported seven hundred miles away to Babylon. There, on the banks of the Kebar River—or what may have been an irrigation canal swinging in a loop southwest from the Euphrates— the Jewish exiles tried to settle. And here, when he was thirty years old and in the fifth year of his exile (about 593 BC, still six years before the destruction of Jerusalem), Ezekiel received an extraordinary vision.

Ezekiel's vision of God reveals something of the character of God. Ezekiel saw God seated on a (mobile) throne seated high above him. He's the King of kings, the sovereign ruler of the universe. Let's recall again that vivid experience with which this Bible book opens. There was:

> *"... a great cloud with fire flashing intermittently and a bright light around it, and in its midst something like gleaming metal in the midst of the fire ... there was something resembling a throne, like lapis lazuli in appearance; and on that which resembled a throne, high up, was a figure with the appearance of a man. Then I noticed from the appearance of His waist and upward something like gleaming metal that looked like fire all around within it, and from the appearance of His waist and downward I saw something like fire; and there was a radiance around Him. Like the appearance of the rainbow in the clouds on a rainy day, so was the appearance of the surrounding radiance. Such was the appearance of the likeness of the glory of the Lord"* (Ezekiel 1:4,26-28).

Another aspect of God's character that's at least indicated in that vision is the holiness of God. Ezekiel doesn't describe God's holiness as much as he brings it out in the powerful symbols he uses. He describes God as surrounded by flashing lightning and bright light (Ezekiel 1:4). *"He looked like glowing metal, as if full of fire . . . and brilliant light surrounded him"* (Ezekiel 1:27). All this shows not only the God who is glorious in holiness, but with it, as events unfolded, also his judgment and wrath.

Now Packer says about the subject of God's wrath: "the modern habit ... is to play the subject down. And that's true even in modern sermons." It's been a long, long time since Jonathan Edwards preached his famous (1741) sermon, "Sinners in the hands of an angry God." The relevance of recalling that is simply this: God will later tell Ezekiel that his wrath must be poured out. God's wrath is nothing like uncontrollable anger. God insists that once his judgment has been meted out, his wrath will then subside and his anger will cease (Ezekiel 5:13). The outbreak of wrath under discussion is, of course, the taking of the Jewish people into captivity. This outbreak forms part of a list of punctuated outbreaks of divine wrath in the Old Testament: there's the Flood, Sodom and Gomorrah, various judgments in the desert (including the wilderness wanderings for forty years), and so on.

The history of God's dealings with his chosen people in the Old Testament may be summed up as Rescue (from Egypt), Residence (by God in the Tabernacle/Temple), Removal and Return (from & to the land). Ezekiel lived at the time of Removal – that of God's people to captivity in Babylon. In those declining times, Ezekiel's call was characterized by three things. First, it was a call to see God and to be humbled. It began with what may have been an actual dust storm but it quickly turns into something supernatural. For Ezekiel soon sees something like glowing metal. Then we have described for us four living creatures who turn out to support the platform of God's throne. In any time when the whole culture is moving in other directions it is essential that those who proclaim the Word of God have their eyes so fastened on what God is like in all his transcendent glory.

Second, for Ezekiel, it's a call to speak God's words and be fearless (Ezekiel 2:3-8). He's to stay 'on message' and not to fudge anything: *"Say to them this is what the sovereign Lord says"* (Ezekiel 2:4). Again verse 6, *"Do not be afraid of them or their words. Do not be afraid. Do not be afraid of what they say, or be terrified by them."* Preachers can be intimidated by their audience and by society's pressure to be politically correct. Preachers don't normally like to get bad reviews. Preaching in declining times takes special courage unlike revival times when it is a joy to go out and preach. When the culture is against you, it takes boldness and resilience.

Perhaps I can mention here that in contrast to God's awesome glory, Ezekiel is addressed as "son of man." It's a phrase that's used around 93 times in the book. Why? It brings out the contrast between a creature in the face of the Creator; between God's eternal character and the brevity of a human lifespan on earth (Psalm 90:2-3). When we've a true vision of God and see him in his glory, we can't help but realize that God is so awesome, and we're essentially dust and can't stand before him. We've already observed the contrast Ezekiel paints between the splendour of God and the ruin of humanity. Here's another contrast - between the transcendent God and the life of humans on earth as something transitory or fleeting. Other prophets major more on this. After speaking of the glory of the LORD that was to be revealed, Isaiah saw the people in his day as grass (chapter 40). Ezekiel, too, is a mere man, but all the same he's to be courageous to speak the words of the eternal God.

Then there's also a third reason why we need our eyes fixed on God in a declining culture. For those of us, in the western world today, where most of the people around us had inherited a Judeo-Christian worldview, it used to be that we could assume everyone already knew the basics that the God we preached was a personal, transcendent being; the intelligent designer of the universe; that there's a difference between right and wrong and truth and error, with God as the final judge; that all sin is finally against God, with "a heaven to be gained and a hell to be shunned"… but we can not assume any more that people know these things.

After the vision, what happens next is interesting. God commands Ezekiel to open his mouth and he'll give him something to eat (Ezekiel 2:8). It's a scroll in fact which is described as containing written lamentations, mourning and woe. In any case, it doesn't sound very appetising, does it? And yet when Ezekiel eats it (Ezekiel 3:3), it tastes sweet as honey in his mouth. That's a shocker! How surprising! How can we relate to this? Well, when we come to bits of the Bible about judgment and doom, we may find ourselves wanting to skip over them because we'd much rather find our favourite, comforting verses. Preachers more and more tend to avoid speaking about such unpleasant things as God's wrath. But Jeremiah (Jeremiah 15:16) and the Apostle John (Revelation 10:8-11) were others who literally had a taste for God's Word. We need preachers who've been with God and known him in his holiness so that for them it's a sweet thing to do his will even when it means delivering a message of judgment.

And so it's a message of judgement Ezekiel has to bring to the people of God in his day. A people in decline. A people rebelling against the knowledge of God. There was no longer any fear of God in their eyes. For to fear the Lord, and to have understanding, is the practical aspect of what knowledge of the Holy One brings (Proverbs 9:10). Packer says: "I walked in the sunshine with a scholar who had effectively forfeited his prospects of academic advancement by clashing with church dignitaries over the gospel of grace. 'But it doesn't matter,' he said at length, 'for I've known God and they haven't.' The remark was a mere parenthesis, a passing comment on something I had said, but it has stuck with me …'[7]

It stuck with me too, and we've focused on the book of the prophet Ezekiel simply because 'knowing God' is the basic theme of this book. We say again that the phrase, *"They – or you - shall know that I am the LORD"* is used around 60 to 70 times in this book. As we've said, the book opens with Ezekiel himself getting a view of God. But in Ezekiel's time the people's view of God had been obscured by other things, as we read: *"And the word of the Lord came to me, saying, "Son of man, these men have set up their idols in their hearts and have put in front of their faces the stumbling block of their wrongdoing. … For anyone of the house of Israel, or of the strangers who reside in Israel, who deserts Me, sets up his idols in his heart, puts in front of his face the stumbling block of his wrongdoing …"* (Ezekiel 14:2-7).

They couldn't see past their idols, the things of their own making. To set up idols in the heart was to separate oneself from the living God (Ezekiel 14:7). And let's be aware that the New Testament plainly says that greed is idolatry or amounts to it (Colossians 3:5). Of course, our governments want us all to be consumers so as to make the economy work. We're constantly encouraged to want more. How many adverts have you seen that tempt you to desire more tasty food, more carefree holidays, more health-care and beauty products? Our secret idol is comfort and physical well-being. We attend church services, but rarely do we pray in private or thoughtfully read

---

[7] *Knowing God*, Chapter 4, The People Who Know Their God

the Word of God. Deep down we are more interested in basking in the sun than we are in basking in the awesome radiance of God's presence.

The Apostle Paul appeals to all Christians down through the centuries to arrive at the same thinking he'd arrived at, namely that knowing Christ is the one thing of surpassing value in life (Philippians 3:8). The nation of Israel – the same as were in decline in Ezekiel's day – will one day share the revised view of Saul of Tarsus. One translation of Hosea 14:8 is: *"Ephraim shall say, 'What have I to do anymore with idols?' I have heard and observed him.'"* This is Israel in the future when even the idols of her own righteousness and of her own clinging to the traditions of her elders will be left behind, and Israel will be altogether taken up with her Messiah and the Word of God. No more "idols of the heart." Then they will know him!

4

A Close Encounter

It was a Tuesday morning and I'd a meeting with a team of scientists from the United States. The date was the 28th of January, 1986. It's etched in my memory because it was the date of the Space Shuttle Challenger disaster. To this day, I distinctly recall how before our meeting with the U.S. scientists began that morning, my immediate superior reached out to the team leader opposite and offered condolences for the loss of the seven astronauts who in exiting gravity had entered eternity. It had been watched live by millions, for only 73 seconds after lift-off from Cape Canaveral, the Space Shuttle had exploded. President Reagan that day gave quite a speech. He talked of "space as the last frontier." And of how "pioneers have always given their lives on the frontier." He later paraphrased a poem by an Air Force volunteer, saying that they "slipped the surly bonds of earth … and touched the face of God."[8]

"Touching God's face" - that's an extremely evocative expression.

---

[8] https://nationalpoetryday.co.uk/poem/high-flight/

It suggests intimacy, as with someone we know well. We come close to God through prayer. In the language of the Bible, we often find expressions such as "seeking God's face." It's a way of describing prayer. And, even more expressive than that, we occasionally come across the still more striking phrase: "the softening of his face," that is literally the softening of God's face (e.g. Exodus 32:11; 1 Kings 13:6; 2 Kings 13:4; Malachi 1:9). That, in turn, may suggest soothing, possibly by touching, and it's an idiom used of a particular type of prayer known as intercessory prayer. We're back to the implied intimacy of touching the face of God. One of the most amazing revelations about God in the Bible is that he wants you and me to become intimate with him.

There are some people among our circle of friends and acquaintances about whom we'd happily say that we're close to them. We find spending time with them to be satisfying and rewarding. But here, we're talking about God. Recently, I began re-reading the Bible again starting from the Book of Genesis and felt I ought to pause when, at chapter 45, I got to the place where Joseph invited his brothers, saying: *"Please come closer"* (Genesis 45:4). That was breath-taking generosity of spirit on the part of Joseph to be able to say that to men who, though they were his own brothers, had horribly betrayed him when he was a youth.

But I found myself thinking of the more breath-taking invitation God gives to sinners through Jesus. *"Come to Me,"* he says. That invitation is the good news of forgiveness that's available from God through Jesus, his son. Then, later in the Bible, this time through the Apostle James (James 4:8), more guidance is given on how believers can draw near to God, perhaps after a time when our behaviours have created some distance. It's as if the Lord is saying 'Please come closer.' The expected response focuses on the need for cleansing, purifying, mourning and humbling ourselves. We've already observed that one of the recurring sins of God's people at the time of the Old Testament prophet, Ezekiel, was idolatry, a problem rooted in the heart of God's people, Israel. They went astray from the heart. God was no longer going to endure this blatant rebellion and rejection of his person. This is what he says in Ezekiel, chapter 14:

"For anyone of the house of Israel, or of the strangers who reside in Israel, who deserts Me, sets up his idols in his heart, puts in front of his face the stumbling block of his wrongdoing, and then comes to the prophet to request something of Me for himself, I the Lord will let Myself answer him Myself. I will set My face against that person and make him a sign and a proverb, and I will eliminate him from among My people. So you will know that I am the Lord" (Ezekiel 14:7,8).

Notice there how God talks about setting his face against them. God was hardening himself against his people's persistent rebelliousness. There was at that time no-one to 'soften his face.' In fact, it'd gone well beyond the reach of intercession, for God went so far as to say that if Noah, Daniel and Job were living then, they'd not deliver any others but only themselves (Ezekiel 14:14). The point is clear: judgement had now become unavoidable. God would deal with his sinning people in wrath so that ultimately they might come to know him. That last part is God's great desire, and it's just one of the more than sixty times that God expresses this purpose through Ezekiel which is that his people should know him. But even in his wrath, God wouldn't go as far as to deal with them as they truly deserved to be punished. After scattering them in judgement, he'd show mercy in bringing them back:

> *"'As I live,' declares the Lord God, 'with a mighty hand and with an outstretched arm and with wrath poured out, I assuredly shall be king over you. I will bring you out from the peoples and gather you from the lands where you are scattered, with a mighty hand and with an outstretched arm and with wrath poured out; and I will bring you into the wilderness of the peoples, and there I will enter into judgment with you face to face. Just as I entered into judgment with your fathers in the wilderness of the land of Egypt, so I will enter into judgment with you,' declares the Lord God ... So you will know that I am the Lord.*
>
> *As for you, house of Israel, this is what the Lord God says: 'Go, serve, everyone of you his idols; but later you will certainly listen to Me, and My holy name you will no longer defile with your gifts and your idols. For on My holy mountain, on the high mountain of Israel," declares the Lord God, "there the entire house of Israel, all of them, will serve Me in the land; there I will accept them and there I will demand your contributions and the choicest of your gifts, with all your holy things.*
>
> *As a soothing aroma I will accept you when I bring you out from the peoples and gather you from the lands where you are scattered; and I will show Myself to be holy among you in the sight of the nations. And you will know that I*

am the Lord, when I bring you into the land of Israel, into the land which I swore to give to your forefathers. And there you will remember your ways and all your deeds by which you have defiled yourselves; and you will loathe yourselves in your own sight for all the evil things that you have done. Then you will know that I am the Lord, when I have dealt with you in behalf of My name, not according to your evil ways or according to your corrupt deeds, house of Israel,' declares the Lord God" (Ezekiel 20:33-44).

God cannot utterly forsake his people. God cannot forget his covenant. God will restore the faithful ones back to the land, back to the worship that will come from their hearts and he will be their God, and they'll be his people. So, the latter part of the book presents God's glory and kingdom as it will return to Israel (chapters 33-48). The holiness of God and sinfulness of his own people are placed side-by-side by Ezekiel. The darkness and awfulness of human sin is presented against the brilliant light of the glory of God. Perhaps, there is no other book in the whole Bible that presents the sins [as in idolatry, bloodshed, desecrating sabbaths ...] of God's people in as much detail as the Book of Ezekiel. Do you want to get the full picture of human sinfulness? Do you want to get the full picture of the awesome character of God and his holiness? Do you want to get the full picture of the wrath of God? In short, do you want to know God? Then study the Book of Ezekiel, and your life will be transformed.

Ezekiel has a two-fold message. On the one hand, he brings a message of judgment. The holiness of God cannot tolerate sin, especially sin in the life of his own people, people who are known by his name. Basically, twenty chapters (4-24) are devoted to presenting this sinfulness. God's wrath is against them because of that. These chapters in the first half of the book, present God's glory in relation to his judging of his people for their sin. But we said Ezekiel has a two-fold message. On the one hand, he brings the message of judgment; on the other hand, Ezekiel brings a message of hope, for God will act for the sake of his name. For his own name's sake, that is based on his own character and nature, he'll allow his face to be softened.

In this way, God's glory is seen in this book in the same two ways as it was seen by the Israelites as they travelled from an earlier captivity in Egypt on their way by the hand of Moses to the border of the promised land. At times then, God's glory was seen in admonition; at other times it was seen in approbation. In other words, to warn or to show approval. To know God is to know his glory in each of these two ways. Israel saw the glory of God in judgement when they murmured against him and complained of hunger in the desert (Exodus 16:10). But they also saw God's glory in a display of satisfaction at times when his commands had been fully kept, for example in the setting up of the Tabernacle and its commencement of operation (Exodus 40; Leviticus 9). In similar ways, Ezekiel saw God's glory retreating from the temple in judgement, but he also saw how the glory of God's gratuitous mercy would return to his people again.

5

Standing Firm

I read about a missionary years ago in the jungles of New Guinea who wrote the following letter to his friends back home:

'Man, it is great to be in the thick of the fight, to draw the old devil's heaviest guns, to have him at you with depression and discouragement, slander, disease. He doesn't waste time on a lukewarm bunch. He hits good and hard when a fellow is hitting him. You can always measure the weight of your blow by the one you get back. When you're on your back with fever and at your last ounce of strength, when some of your converts backslide, when you learn that your most promising inquirers are only fooling, when your mail gets held up, and some don't bother to answer your letters, is that the time to put on mourning? No sir. That's the time to pull out the stops and shout Hallelujah! The [Devil's] getting it in the neck and hitting back. Heaven is leaning over the battlements and watching. "Will he stick with it?" As they see who is with us, as they see the unlimited reserves, the boundless resources, as they see the impossibility of failure, how disgusted and sad they must be when we run away. Glory to God! We're not going to run away. We're going to stand!' (Bible.org)

That was a guy who was standing firm. And that's what I want to talk about now. The Apostle Paul seemed to love that little expression: *"to stand firm."* Some Bible versions have him using it about ten times (twice in his Corinthian letters; once to the Galatians; three times to Ephesus; twice to Philippi; and, finally, twice to the Thessalonians). He uses it to pass on the charge to *"stand firm"* in the knowledge of Christ, by, for example, not yielding to false teachings.

"Stand firm!" It's the language of the battle line. Many movies depict ancient warfare as involving people fighting in a chaotic fashion, relying on their wits and their skill with weapons to fight off a sequence of individual combatants. This may make for good cinema, but it's not really historically accurate and doesn't give us a true impression of what was meant by standing firm as a soldier. Most armies in Bible times were largely made up of unskilled conscripts, with a nucleus of the few trained soldiers that made up the king's bodyguard. However, as a result of the conscripts adding to the size of the formations, they still played an important part in the battle. Very few died in actual combat back then; the majority of casualties occurred when one side gave in to fear and tried to flee. This provoked a chase and the slaughter of those who were running away. Therefore the role of a common soldier in an army wasn't to kill hundreds of the opposition, but to stand firm and not give in to fear – to keep panic from spreading through the whole army and putting everyone in danger.

With that in mind, let's look at Paul's use of the command "to stand firm." There's a lot bound up in that little word - stand. First of all, it means that we're going to come under attack and we mustn't be frightened. It means that we mustn't droop or slouch, being uncertain or half-hearted in the fight (no self-pity is allowed). It means that we're to be at our position and alert. It means that we don't give even a moment's thought to retreating. But, let's think about why we're exploring this idea. Remember, we're in a series of studies about what it means to know God. There's a statement in the Book of Daniel that says: *"the people who know their God will be strong and take action"* (Daniel 11:32). In other words, those who truly know God, even if they're faced with the most difficult circumstances against overwhelming odds – as the missionary in our opening anecdote was – they will be resolute (or "firm") and still achieve things for God.

The Apostle Paul's repeated encouragement to others to stand firm has great authenticity because he was someone who truly knew God. We only need to think of the exalted thoughts he expresses in his letters when he writes to the churches about the person of Christ; or the boldness with which he fearlessly preaches the Gospel even before kings and judges; or the deep contentment he demonstrates in challenging circumstances; and, not least, the tireless energy with which he serves God in the Gospel. Paul knew the Lord and his personal desire in life was to know him even better.

We learn from Paul's writings in the Bible that our standing is in the Lord, in his grace, his will, in the Gospel, and the Faith. God gives the Christian believer on the Lord Jesus a glorious standing which he or she is to maintain by warring the spiritual warfare. To quote Paul from various places: We stand in grace (Romans 5:2); we stand in the gospel (1 Corinthians 15:1); we stand in courage and strength (1 Corinthians 16:13); we stand in faith (2 Corinthians 1:24); we stand in Christian liberty (Galatians 5:1); we stand in Christian unity (Philippians 1:27); we stand in the Lord (Philippians 4:1; 1 Thessalonians 3:8); and we should stand perfect and complete in the will of God (Colossians 4:12).

So, we're not to retreat, not to yield ground. We're to hold position. Having done everything, we're to stand firm. This sorts out those who truly know their God. When opposition comes, it's those who know their God who stand firm. Around the world, believers are facing extreme times of persecution or are caught in the cross-hairs of an oppressive regime or are required to hold their nerve when hostile legislation is passed targeting them. But all these things involve flesh and blood. That's not the real battlefront. Behind all the malevolent moves by humans on earth are spiritual forces directing them. This is what Paul tells us in the sixth chapter of his letter to the Ephesians. In the opening of that letter that celebrates our position "in Christ," he's told us that we're really blessed, and that those blessings are in the heavenly realms. But when he closes the same letter, he informs us that it's from those same heavenly realms that our opposition comes. He says:

> *"Finally, be strong in the Lord and in the strength of His might. Put on the full armor of God, so that you will be able to stand firm against the schemes of the devil. For our struggle is not against flesh and blood, but against the rulers, against the powers, against the world forces of*

this darkness, against the spiritual forces of wickedness in the heavenly places. Therefore, take up the full armor of God, so that you will be able to resist on the evil day, and having done everything, to stand firm.

Stand firm therefore, having belted your waist with truth, and having put on the breastplate of righteousness, and having strapped on your feet the preparation of the gospel of peace; in addition to all, taking up the shield of faith with which you will be able to extinguish all the flaming arrows of the evil one. And take the helmet of salvation and the sword of the Spirit, which is the word of God. With every prayer and request, pray at all times in the Spirit" (Ephesians 6:10-18).

Did you notice that no less than three times, he says *"stand firm."* We're not to attempt to go careering off on any foolish offensive. We're simply to hold our ground. C. S. Lewis said that Satan doesn't mind whether we totally ignore him or we're totally obsessed by him. Either way is fine by him because either way opens it up for him to do exactly what he wants to do. Those who are totally obsessed by Satan, quite frankly, are paranoid. They see him lurking everywhere. On the other hand, those who are totally ignorant of Satan — those who simply ignore him or don't even believe he exists ... Either way he does his work.

F. F. Bruce said that Satan's main activity is putting obstacles in the path of the people of God to prevent the will of God from being accomplished in and through them. If some people are obsessed by Satan they're not doing anything; they're paralyzed, so he's won. Other people who totally ignore Satan don't even recognize what he's doing, so they have no idea what's happening. One of the great mysteries of the Christian faith is that God in his sovereign purposes allows the enemy of souls and the enemy of his purposes to continue his work, but it's all under divine permission. So, it's powerful and permitted, but real nevertheless.

Those in the Church at Thessalonica, were facing persecution. Paul says to them: *"So then, brothers and sisters, stand firm and hold on to the traditions which you were taught, whether by word of mouth or by letter from us"* (2 Thessalonians 2:15). One of Paul's major concerns about sending Timothy to Thessalonica was that in some way the tempter might have tempted them. Satan puts very tempting opportunities in front of us which, if we go through with them, will deliver us to spiritual shipwreck. Yet every temptation to go wrong is also an opportunity to do right. That's why, when you read in the New Testament about temptation and testing, the same Greek word is translated as temptation *or* testing. A temptation becomes a test when, instead of succumbing to the temptation, you say 'no' and come out stronger. That's why we need to encourage each other to stand firm.

The Apostle Paul says that he sent Timothy to strengthen and encourage the Thessalonians in the faith so that none would be unsettled by their trials. They were having a very difficult time. Paul, understanding their physical danger, the psychological stress, the personal anxiety, understanding they are young believers without adequate leadership, also wanted to make sure that even with everything stacked against them they will stand firm in the faith. Believers in the Church of God at Corinth had been infiltrated by false teachers who were teaching against bodily resurrection (chapter 15), Paul says to the loyal church: *"Be on the alert, stand firm in the faith, act like men, be strong"* (1 Corinthians 16:13). Let's be sure to do likewise!

6

Becoming Sanctified

The Book of Proverbs (Proverbs 9:10; 30:3) makes mention, at least twice, of the knowledge of the Holy One. That's not at all surprising, since the grand theme of that book is wisdom and understanding. Isaiah was given a vision of the Holy One. He saw him with six-winged angels or seraphim surrounding his throne in heaven and there they were shouting to one another *"holy, holy, holy."* In Bible times and languages, when repetition was used it was a device used for emphasis that compares with our devices of underlining a word, or emboldening it, or adding an exclamation mark. I think we've got to assume that God was communicating in terms that would be clearly understood at that time on earth. In other words, this had the effect of proclaiming that the Lord is very, very, holy. That's how Isaiah would have understood it.

The Apostle John had a similar vision into heaven. What he saw and heard is recorded in Revelation 4, verses 8 and 11: *"And the four living creatures ... say, 'HOLY, HOLY, HOLY IS THE LORD GOD, THE ALMIGHTY, who was and who is and who is to come.'"*

The four living creatures once again address God as *"Holy, holy, holy."* And we remind ourselves that the primary meaning of that word 'holy' is otherness or difference. Although it does have the thought of moral purity, it first of all has the thought of God's otherness. God is holy and knowledge of the Holy One therefore immediately impresses on us that God is different. Now the name of God, as distinct from his titles, is related to the verb 'to be', as in 'The Great I Am.' And so here we have God described as the One who was and who is and who ever will be. This begins to show us just how different God is from us, and from any other 'being.'

Then we come down to verse 11, where the 24 elders say, *"Worthy are You our Lord and our God, to receive glory and honor and power, for You created all things, and because of Your will they existed, and were created."* Between these two verses, verses eight and 11 of Revelation chapter four, we've brought before us the fundamental difference between God and us, between God and anyone or anything else. God is the everlasting 'I AM', the ever-existing One. We all had a beginning, and he was responsible for it. Down through history, Christian thinkers have spoken of God, not only as the Supreme Being, but as a necessary being. What does that mean? It means God simply must be, or putting it differently with a double negative: God is the only being who simply cannot not be. Because if God should cease to exist, the entire universe would vaporize and disappear.

Looking at that the other way around, people have seen a classic argument for the existence of God. Because suppose God did not exist; suppose once there was absolutely nothing - that is, not anything, not even a sea of energy, no scientific laws, absolutely nothing, then there would still now be absolutely nothing - because there is no such thing as a free lunch. You simply cannot get something out of nothing, not spontaneously, and equally not in 20 billion years. To say otherwise, and to believe otherwise, is to believe in magic. In fact, it's even worse than that. It would be like pulling a rabbit out of a hat without the hat, and without the magician. In verse 11 of Revelation 4, the 24 elders are worshipping God, and they're saying "because of you all things were created, and because of your sovereign will they began to exist." God and God alone has the prerogative of bringing something out of nothing. There's no other logical or scientific explanation; let all enquiry cease, and worship begin. God's words, "I am the LORD and there is no other", also formed the introduction to himself that God gave a pagan king in history. This was a king God had singled out for a very special purpose:

> *"This is what the Lord says to Cyrus His anointed,*
>   *Whom I have taken by the right hand,*
>   *To subdue nations before him ...,*
>   *So that you may know that it is I,*
>   *The Lord, the God of Israel, who calls you by your name.*
>   *"For the sake of Jacob My servant,*
>   *And Israel My chosen one,*
>   *I have also called you by your name;*
>   *I have given you a title of honor*
>   *Though you have not known Me.*
>   *"I am the Lord, and there is no one else;*
>   *There is no God except Me.*
>   *I will arm you, though you have not known Me,*
>   *So that people may know from the rising to the setting*

> *of the sun*
> > *That there is no one besides Me.*
> > *I am the Lord, and there is no one else,*
> > *The One forming light and creating darkness,*
> > *Causing well-being and creating disaster;*
> > *I am the Lord who does all these things"* (Isaiah 45:1-7).

Before the chapter is finished, God will have repeated at least ten times *"there is no one else,"* no God except him, no one besides him – or words to that effect. God acknowledges that this man, the Persian king, Cyrus, to whom he's in the process of revealing himself is someone who's not known him. Despite that, God had selected him (about 100 years in the future) to be his chosen instrument so that all peoples from east to west in the whole world would come to know the true God who is without equal. He simply 'is', and there is no other. In other words, God is holy, meaning there's none like him. And nothing at all happens in this world – whether good or bad – without God at least permitting it to happen.

What we've been establishing so far, is that knowing God is to know the Holy One, and we're talking about knowledge of one who is utterly unique. And yet, God says to Christian believers through the Apostle Peter in the New Testament: *"You shall be holy, for I am holy"* (1 Peter 1:16). This is the process that the Bible describes as sanctification. It's about us becoming different from our old self, from our environment all around us, and becoming Christ-like - like God himself. And, of course, it's the work of God. It involves the application of the death of Christ and the Bible, as well as the activity of the Holy Spirit. In one sense, of course, we've already been made holy as soon as we became a believer on the Lord Jesus, but in an ongoing day-to-day sense we're intended to become in practical Christian living what we already are in God's eyes through the death of Christ. This reminds us of the Church of God at Corinth where the Apostle Paul addressed them as 'saints,' that is sanctified ones made holy in Christ by their saving faith, but soon went on to criticise them for their unholy behaviours such as envy and strife. This process of practical sanctification is gradual, and sometimes painful, as the writer to the Hebrews says:

> *"Furthermore, we had earthly fathers to discipline us, and we respected them; shall we not much more be subject to the Father of spirits, and live? For they disciplined us for a short time as seemed best to them, but He disciplines us for our good, so that we may share His holiness"* (Hebrews 12:9,10).

Notice that God's aim, should he have to discipline us, is to maximise the degree to which we share his holiness. But, remember, God's holiness is saying something very profound about his nature, his being. It's no surprise then that the Apostle Peter gives us a tutorial on how we can become sharers or partakers of the divine nature, even as we become sharers of his holiness. In the statements that follow him saying that, he explains this wonderful mystery in a series of very practical steps that again stress what it really means to know God:

> *"... [God's] power has granted to us everything pertaining to life and godliness, through the true knowledge of Him who called us by His own glory and excellence. Through these He has granted to us His precious and magnificent*

promises, so that by them you may become partakers of the divine nature, having escaped the corruption that is in the world on account of lust. Now for this very reason also, applying all diligence, in your faith supply moral excellence, and in your moral excellence, knowledge, and in your knowledge, self-control, and in your self-control, perseverance, and in your perseverance, godliness, and in your godliness, brotherly kindness, and in your brotherly kindness, love.

For if these qualities are yours and are increasing, they do not make you useless nor unproductive in the true knowledge of our Lord Jesus Christ. For the one who lacks these qualities is blind or short-sighted, having forgotten his purification from his former sins. Therefore, brothers and sisters, be all the more diligent to make certain about His calling and choice of you; for as long as you practice these things, you will never stumble; for in this way the entrance into the eternal kingdom of our Lord and Savior Jesus Christ will be abundantly supplied to you" (2 Peter 1:3-11).

If we are keen to supply these qualities in our living here for God, then we will increasingly experience what it means to know God and will find him using us. We'll also be confident Christians in the right sense, not tripping over ourselves, and – as my old Bible teacher used to say – we'll enter the eternal kingdom like an old-time sailing ship 'under full sail.'

7

A Compassionate King

A police officer [somewhere in the U.S.] pulled a driver aside and asked for his license and registration. "What's wrong, officer?" the driver asked. "I didn't go through any red lights, and I certainly wasn't speeding." "No, you weren't," said the officer, "but I saw you waving your fist as you swerved around the lady driving in the left lane. I further observed your flushed and angry face as you shouted at the driver of the Hummer who cut you off, and how you pounded your steering wheel when the traffic came to a stop near the bridge." "Is that a crime, officer?" "No, but when I saw the 'Jesus loves you and so do I' bumper sticker on the car, I figured this car had to be stolen."[9]

Mmm, I wonder. It's hard to live the Christian life with total integrity, isn't it? We sympathise with the Apostle Paul in Romans chapter 7, where he confesses he sometimes did the very things he didn't want to do. But, it's plain to see

---

[9] Adapted from Homiletics magazine (May 2004); submitted by Gino Grunberg, Gig Harbor, Washington.

that Paul was troubled by that inconsistency. On the other hand, it would seem the Jewish religious leaders, known as the Pharisees, whom our Lord charged with being hypocrites, weren't troubled at all. The fact they were being inconsistent seemed to go right under their radar, meaning they either didn't or scarcely noticed it. As Christians, we make big claims; they're faith claims - we say we belong to God and that we're citizens of heaven. But how well does our life measure up to these claims? That was the challenge the Apostle John addressed in his first letter:

> "If we say that we have no sin, we are deceiving ourselves and the truth is not in us. If we confess our sins, He is faithful and righteous, so that He will forgive us our sins and cleanse us from all unrighteousness. If we say that we have not sinned, we make Him a liar and His word is not in us. My little children, I am writing these things to you so that you may not sin. And if anyone sins, we have an Advocate with the Father, Jesus Christ the righteous; and He Himself is the propitiation for our sins …
>
> By this we know that we have come to know Him, if we keep His commandments. The one who says, "I have come to know Him," and does not keep His commandments, is a liar, and the truth is not in him; but whoever follows His word, in him the love of God has truly been perfected. By this we know that we are in Him: the one who says that he remains in Him ought, himself also, to walk just as He walked" *(1 John 1:8–2:6).*

In other words, John says that the way we assure ourselves that we really know the Lord is if we keep his commandments. John was dealing with people who were making claims about themselves that couldn't be justified. Some were saying they had no sins in their life, and that they'd come to know the Lord, perhaps implying they had a knowledge of God that was in advance of that of others. The Apostle John lost no time in bursting their bubble. If they didn't live like Christ, then they did not know him. And in claiming to be sinless, well, they were simply self-deceived. However, in his letter John does give us three tests of authentic belief. We assure ourselves, in the first place, that our faith claims are real if and when we sustain our doctrinal beliefs, especially about the person of Christ; and when we do what's right and keep his commandments; and thirdly, when we love others, especially our fellow Christians.

In the Old Testament, it seems the prophet Jeremiah was facing a similar issue. Some belonging to the Old Testament community of God's people, were making big claims, even boasting. Jeremiah, the prophet, brings them God's message:

> *"This is what the Lord says: 'Let no wise man boast of his wisdom, nor let the mighty man boast of his might, nor a rich man boast of his riches; but let the one who boasts boast of this, that he understands and knows Me, that I am the Lord who exercises mercy, justice, and righteousness on the earth; for I delight in these things,' declares the Lord"* (Jeremiah 9:23,24).

All other boasting is futile. It's the same today. Some people flaunt their intelligence. The term 'The world's most powerful man' gets thrown around, usually with reference to the American President. For others, it's about getting on the Forbes' list of America's richest people. Jeremiah says don't even go there. That's not where it's at, not even close. There is one thing to rejoice in and that is if you know God! In this sense, it really is about who you know. And those who truly know God – for whom the claim is no fake claim – know that he specialises in mercy and justice and righteousness. These things are in scarce supply in today's world, which must go to show that the movers and shakers on the planet today have a deep ignorance of God. That's nothing to boast about, but only to be pitied.

The Apostle Paul would boast in nothing else other than the cross of Christ. Two thousand years ago, the rulers of this world had no knowledge of the Lord of glory, and so they crucified him. It won't always be this way. The time is coming when the knowledge of the Lord will cover the earth as the waters cover the sea. There's a song that takes up these biblical words, and my friend Mario in the Philippines loves to go around singing them. He's got no power or wealth to boast in, but he does know God.

We're thinking about knowing God, about what it means to say we know God. Talking about world leaders and powerful men, God, through Jeremiah, contrasts two of them. They're father and son, and both were Judean kings of southern Israel. He begins with a description of the current king, Jehoiakim, and goes on to remind him of the contrasting lifestyle of his father, King Josiah:

> *"Woe to him who builds his house without righteousness,*

And his upstairs rooms without justice,
Who uses his neighbor's services without pay
And does not give him his wages,
Who says, 'I will build myself a large house
With spacious upstairs rooms,
And cut out its windows,
Paneling it with cedar and painting it bright red.'
"Do you become a king because you are competing in cedar?
Did your father not eat and drink
And do justice and righteousness?
Then it was well for him.
"He pled the cause of the afflicted and the poor,
Then it was well.
Is that not what it means to know Me?"
Declares the Lord.
"But your eyes and your heart
Are intent only upon your own dishonest gain,
And on shedding innocent blood,
And on practicing oppression and extortion."
Therefore this is what the Lord says regarding Jehoiakim the son of Josiah, king of Judah:
"They will not mourn for him:
'Oh, my brother!' or, 'Oh, sister!'
They will not mourn for him:
'Oh, for the master!' or, 'Oh, for his splendor!'
"He will be buried with a donkey's burial,
Dragged off and thrown out beyond the gates of Jerusalem.

(Jeremiah 22:13-19)

That's a most illuminating commentary of the lives of these two men. Illuminating for this reason: it says very plainly what it means to know God, what the essence of it is, and so how such a claim by anyone to know God can be tested for authenticity – or dismissed as hypocrisy. To know God is to act with justice and righteousness, and to plead the cause of those who are less privileged and who are experiencing any kind of affliction. Sadly, the king at that time, Jehoiakim, was intent on dishonest gain, spilling innocent blood and engaged in the oppression and extortion of his own people. God was unknown to him. We can take away the personal challenge: how well do I know God? Can it be said of my life that I *"do justly, love mercy, and walk humbly with my God?"* (Micah 6:8). I remember a believer in Ireland who whenever he was replying to a friendly greeting asking 'How are you doing?' He'd reply, with a twinkle in his eye, 'Oh, I'm doing justly …'

8

Living Your Best Life

There's a saying which goes something like 'the good is the enemy of the best.' What I think that's meant to convey is this: that settling for something satisfactory or 'OK' is one of the main reasons we often don't press on for even better results, for excellence. This applies, too, in spiritual things. People talk about being in their 'comfort zone.' Who would not be reluctant to leave a comfortable, respectable situation? Many Christians avoid obvious failure. They seem to be doing all right. They conform to the norms of Christian respectability. They settle for what seems practical and realistic. Perhaps that seems reasonable, until you read again Paul's letter to the Philippians - a letter that challenges us to leave behind all that's mundane and mediocre in our Christian experience. The letter resonates with the gospel as being the single passion of Paul's life. In his hands everything turns to the gospel – even when he's in prison. Prison-life opens doors to new captive audiences! The gospel is always bigger than his personal circumstances, and he even manages to glory in his chains.

And if the gospel is the single passion of his life, then knowing Christ is the steady pursuit of his life. For Paul, Christianity is all about relationship – a relationship with Jesus Christ, the son of God - a relationship that grows closer with the passing years of life's varied experiences. The language of the text of this Bible letter invites us to picture Paul like an athlete who's always trying to improve on his personal best – here it's an athletic pursuit of Christlikeness. Ever onward and upward, he steadily pursues a more intimate knowledge of the heart and will of Christ. Rather than waste time complaining about his circumstances, Paul's focus was fixed on how he could advance his appreciation of Christ through these experiences.

And if the gospel is his **single passion**; and a deepening personal relationship with the son of God is his **steady pursuit**; then the **sole purpose** of his life is to live in conformity with the cross of Christ; in other words, to follow a lifestyle in keeping with the God who in Christ sacrificed himself on the cross – such a lifestyle will always be centred on others, and not be about acquiring material possessions. Instead, it'll be a downwardly mobile lifestyle, characterized by the giving of one's own self for the advantage of others. Paul was never a man to rest on his laurels. He just kept on pressing forward. That's a good example for us to follow. Whatever stage of Christian maturity we've reached – or think we have – we must never think we've got as far as we're going to get. The aims and ambitions Paul had for his own life were ones he warmly commended to his friends at Philippi. To be assured of that, let's take the time to listen again to how Paul, after beginning his letter with his customary introduction, quickly shares the substance of his praying for them:

"And this is my prayer: that your love may abound more and more in knowledge and depth of insight, so that you may be able to discern what is best and may be pure and blameless until the day of Christ, filled with the fruit of righteousness that comes through Jesus Christ— to the glory and praise of God" (Philippians 1:9-11 NIV).

Life, at least in some parts of the world today, is full of choices. We choose between different options. Some options are good, only one is best. As it is with us today, two thousand years ago people faced choices. At the heart of this simple and short prayer for his friends, was Paul's request that they might *"discern what is best."* In the choices which confronted them then, they had to prove or test the differing options and decide upon the one that was best. Paul prayed that they might be divinely guided in that lifestyle choice. What's more we can be clear this choice was something which would set the moral tone of their lives. We can be sure of this because Paul prayed that their *"love may abound more and more in knowledge and depth of insight, so that you may be able to discern what is best and may be pure and blameless."*

Getting the best out of life, discovering what they should devote themselves to, demanded they first come to abound in love that was in accord with knowledge and insight. Some of us are rather prone to make choices based on a kind of slushy sentimentalism. That's not the sort of love Paul's talking about here. Going in for the best thing in life is to be based on an increasing love, a love that's consistent with knowledge and moral insight, and which would result in them being pure and blameless.

This selection of what's best is also just as clearly a decision with long-term consequences. For Paul brings in the values of eternity: an eternity which will already have dawned upon us when we stand before Christ and he assesses our service at his tribunal or judgement-seat. Paul's prayer here anticipates that time and its concern is that they – and we - should live now in the light of that coming day. So what was this best option which Paul prayed they might discern and choose for themselves? I'll tell you what I believe it was. Near the end of the letter Paul says: *"Whatever you have learned or received or heard from me, or seen in me— put it into practice"* (Philippians 4:9 NIV).

That's quite some statement – by God's grace Paul lived what he preached. So it was right for them to imitate him, even as he imitated Christ. In the whole context of this letter, as Paul shares his own single passion, his steady pursuit, and what was the sole purpose of his life, do we not see the very thing modelled which is the best choice in life – the only worthy pursuit of a lifetime? Can we too not *"discern what is best,"* namely to: *"... want to know Christ and the power of his resurrection and the fellowship of sharing in his sufferings, becoming like him in his death ... press[ing] on to take hold of that for which Christ Jesus took hold of me"* (Philippians 3:10-12 NIV)?

Is that not the best thing we could ever pray for? I wonder what percentage of our praying involves asking God for good health or recovery from illness; for safety on the roads; a good job; success in exams; the needs of our children; success in our mortgage application or job promotion interview; and much more of the same? All of these are perfectly valid prayer concerns, but as you read through the prayers of the apostle

Paul as they are recorded for us in the Bible you can't help but notice that things like these are not, shall we say, the focus of Paul's praying.

We've thought about prayer requests in which we often ask God for recovery from illness; for safety on the roads; success in job promotion interviews – that kind of thing. But of all the requests we direct to God in prayer, we could ask ourselves 'which of them will make any difference a billion years from now?' I know that raises all sorts of issues about eternity being outside of space and time and all that, but I hope you get my point all the same – it's got to do with the importance of our prayers from an eternal perspective. Whether or not I got the promotion I was chasing will soon pale into total insignificance over against whether I lived a life worthy of the calling to be a Christian. It's that issue that'll be key when Jesus Christ examines the quality of our life of service at his judgement-seat tribunal.

When we see all the biblical examples of Paul's praying we ought to get the message that our priority in praying should not be that we might become successful or wealthy or healthy or happy, or even that all our problems might disappear. This prayer fits in with so much New Testament teaching, teaching which basically urges us to become what we are. By that I mean we're to live out in practice, and in public, what God has already made us to be in his sight and by his grace. For example, through faith we are made righteous before God, that is we're given a right standing before him. Now, as Christians, we're called upon to live righteously - in other words to choose right actions instead of wrong ones. Again through God's grace in Christ, and by means of the faith he's granted us, we're no longer sinners in God's sight but we've been made holy in Christ. As a result, the Bible commands Christians to live increasingly holy lives – others observing us should be able to see a practical difference as old sinful patterns of behaviour fall away.

It's a challenge to us to think how often we pray this prayer of Paul – for ourselves, for our family or church friends. Is it true that we tend to spend more time and energy praying that we, our children and friends will pass exams, get good jobs, and recover health rather than praying that they live lives worthy of what it means to be a Christian. And widening it slightly, what about our general aspirations for those we love? Sometimes when families meet, they exchange news about how their children are doing. Often the news that's shared may be in terms of "Oh, our Susan's getting married to a lovely fella. He's a partner in a law firm that's doing really well. Her own career as a research scientist is really taking off too, so it's an exciting time for her! And Johnny's [that's her brother] into computing, you know - top of his university year group he is. And what's more, he's already got a top job lined up. What did you say? Spiritually? Oh, I see, you mean to ask how they're getting on spiritually – well, they travel a lot you know, and Johnny particularly is not really walking with the Lord right now. But we're sure it's just a phase he's going through."

Perhaps such a parent is only being positive in the meantime, but how do these values appear in eternity's perspective? When we stand before the Lord in glory the only issue will be if we've lived a life worthy of our Christian calling, whether we've lived for Christ and for God's Kingdom and its values. Nothing else will matter. Now, how's that thought going to shift the balance and focus of our prayer-life?

9

Outwards from the Innermost

I remember an interview with a Jewish rabbi in which he said he knew what the middle word of their Bible was – that being, of course, the Old Testament part of today's standard evangelical Bible. It wasn't that he was boasting. He explained that for him this was quite natural because he viewed it as a love letter from God. He asked if this wasn't what anyone did with a love letter: the recipient would analyse every single word, enjoying the selection.

I was reminded of that again the other day when it was pointed out to me that the description of the Day of Atonement ('yom kippur') is central to the Book of Leviticus. This was based on it being the 19th of 37 sayings of God throughout the book. But, more than that, there's a feature of Hebrew (biblical) literature that supports that. The layout of the major themes in the book [sanctuary worship (offerings & festivals) chapters 1-7 & 23-27; priests chapters 8-10 & 21-22; purity chapters 11-15 & 17-20] forms a mirror image of itself with the account of the Day of Atonement in the centrefold, as it were.

The Day of Atonement was of central importance to the community life of God's ancient people in service for him. Their continuing corporate worship of the God of heaven depended on it. This was because the sins and impurities of the people acted as spiritually toxic contaminants. At this time, God lived in a tent (known as the Tabernacle) that was placed central to the encampment of his people as they travelled through the desert to the land he'd promised to their forefathers. I said, God's visible presence was central to his people. However, because God is the holy God of heaven, and he was interacting with a sinful people on this fallen earth, there had to be, as it were, various 'buffer zones' between God and his people as they – at least representatively – drew near before their God. God's holiness and human sin just don't mix, but are quite incompatible. God's detailed instructions to Moses throughout the Book of Leviticus were all about making that crystal clear in the most graphic way.

Let's try to visualise that with a sort of bird's eye view back then, or imagining we'd travelled back in time with a modern drone. We begin out in the desert remoteness, with the entire encampment in the distance. We fly in until we come to a surrounding area which can be designated as 'outside (of) the camp.' Venturing further, we travel over a portion of the well-ordered groupings of the tribes with all the individual household tents of the families belonging to them. Our flyover now brings us to courtyard of the place, acting as a portable temple, where God lived among his people. The border here is very clearly marked with high and bright imposing screens with just one colourful gate as its entrance. What first dominates this courtyard is an altar with smoke ascending skywards from sacrifices burning on it, being officiated by priests. But next we come to the portable tented structure itself, known as the tabernacle proper.

At this point, it's necessary to switch on our drone's X-ray capability. This allows us to detect that the tented structure we've mentioned has a partition boundary inside that makes it into two rooms: an outer and an inner. The Bible often refers to just the outer one as 'the tent of meeting' and it has some furniture, notably a small incense altar. To go further, we're in danger of intruding into the inner space where only one man in those times was authorised to boldly go – that is, into the immediate presence of the holy God. That holy place is characterised by the Ark of the Covenant. Directly above that stood a radiant cloud rising like a pillar and depicting to these people the presence of their God who was in residence there. This was very or most holy territory, and we've only been able to access it by proceeding through these many distinct buffer zones, each graded on a scale of holiness as we might suppose, after having come from the remote – and as it were profane – spaces of the solitary desert, far removed from any fellowship with the holy God seemingly secluded in the innermost part of this portable temple.

On missionary travels to various countries in Africa and Asia, I've sometimes watched as someone, and typically it's been a woman, swept the dust out from the family home. Using a primitive brush, she starts deep within the simple house until she makes her way to the doorway, sweeping out the cloud of dust. And then she continues brushing and sweeping the small front yard and out through the gap in the hedge. Even there, she doesn't stop but keeps on brushing the flat earth until the dust is finally swept away into the surrounding vegetation or bush. Now listen to a few verses from Leviticus chapter 16 that summarise the annual ritual of the most important day in Israel's calendar year:

> *"When he finishes atoning for the Holy Place and the tent of meeting and the altar, he shall offer the live goat. Then Aaron shall lay both of his hands on the head of the live goat, and confess over it all the wrongdoings of the sons of Israel and all their unlawful acts regarding all their sins; and he shall place them on the head of the goat and send it away into the wilderness by the hand of a man who stands ready. Then the goat shall carry on itself all their wrongdoings to an isolated territory; he shall release the goat in the wilderness. "Then Aaron shall come into the tent of meeting and take off the linen garments which he put on when he went into the Holy Place, and shall leave them there. And he shall bathe his body with water in a holy place and put on his clothes, and come out and offer his burnt offering and the burnt offering of the people, and make atonement for himself and for the people. Then he shall offer up in smoke the fat of the sin offering on the altar"* (Leviticus 16:20-25).

Can you see any parallel with my observation of the lady sweeping the dust out from her home? I mentioned how she started deep within and made her way progressively until beyond the edge of what she considered to be belonging to her. Here, we read how Aaron, the high priest of Israel, first atoned for or cleansed the Holy Place of God's immediate presence innermost in the tent. Next mentioned is the fact that he atoned for or cleansed the tent of meeting (which was the next zone, moving outwards). Then there's mention of the altar outside in the courtyard at which the entire courtyard area was atoned for or cleansed. The remains of the animal sacrifices that day were burned *"outside the camp"* (v.27). And there was also a 'scapegoat,' a goat that wasn't ceremonially killed but was directed out into the remote and solitary desert way beyond the outside place surrounding the camp. It went, never to return, away into the far distance symbolically bearing the sins of the people.

Do you see how this was a systematic cleansing from deep within to the furthest extremity? As we've looked into the Book of Ezekiel, we've already seen that the holiness of God can't coexist with human sin. We saw them spoken of side by side in the text of our Bibles there, but then we watched with the prophet Ezekiel as the glory of the holy God progressively abandoned his temple in the midst of his people; and God's judgement fell upon his sinning people by removing them far away into exile in a spiritual desert. We've also had our attention drawn previously to both Isaiah's and the Apostle John's glimpse into heaven. Surely the biggest thing that struck them as they recorded their experiences was the utter holiness of the divine being. God is a holy God. Knowledge of God is knowledge of the Holy One. God's holiness is first and foremost the quality of God that sets him apart. He's not like us. He's holy, other, different.

But amazingly God wants contact with us and wants us to approach him in worship. He's done everything to make this possible. The writer of the New Testament letter to the

Hebrews explains the relevance of Leviticus chapter 16 to people everywhere today. There we read:

"... it was necessary for the copies of the things in the heavens to be cleansed with these things, but the heavenly things themselves with better sacrifices than these. For Christ did not enter a holy place made by hands, a mere copy of the true one, but into heaven itself, now to appear in the presence of God for us; nor was it that He would offer Himself often, as the high priest enters the Holy Place year by year with blood that is not his own. Otherwise, He would have needed to suffer often since the foundation of the world; but now once at the consummation of the ages He has been revealed to put away sin by the sacrifice of Himself. And just as it is destined for people to die once, and after this comes judgment, so Christ also, having been offered once to bear the sins of many, will appear a second time for salvation without reference to sin, to those who eagerly await Him" (Hebrews 9:23-28).

God was picturing ultimate realities for us by using these Old Testament rituals. There is a reality in heaven where sinners who have been forgiven through the sacrifice of God's son, Jesus, on the cross, can draw near to express their gratitude to the infinitely holy God. Even if we believe we're following the Lord Jesus' instructions as we draw near among his people to worship him in heaven each week, we must always remain conscious that we live in a defiling world and the God we come to is a consuming fire. Secure in Christ, as blood-bought through his death, we still come respectfully and tread softly with reverent fear for the God we worship is awesome beyond anything we can appreciate! What an unspeakable privilege that we can know this God through the person and work of Jesus Christ, his son!

10

From Eternity to Eternity

The Apostle Paul wrote to Christians in Galatia and made a contrast between the *"... time when you did not know God, ...* [and] *... now that you have come to know God, or rather to be known by God"* (Galatians 4:8,9). Until this point in our studies, we've been focussing on the amazing wonder of what it means for someone to know God. Might it not be true to say that there's only one thing greater than that? And what might that be? What could be greater than knowing the creator of the universe? It is, I suggest, to be known by him.

We could never know royalty unless they chose to take notice of us and were to draw us into their circle of friends. Those who are born and raised far off from the palaces of this world have little or no chance of making their way inside that world of privilege. And so it's as if Paul checks himself when he speaks of the Galatian believers having come to know God; and he qualifies that quickly, adding *"or rather* [have come] *to be known by God."* To the Christians at Rome, he wrote: *"... we have peace with God through our Lord Jesus Christ, through whom we also have obtained our introduction by faith into this grace in which we stand; and we celebrate in hope of the glory of God"* (Romans 5:1,2). It's all by God's grace, his sovereign grace from before the world began, that we can come to know God. Paul wrote to the Corinthian Christians and could say to them:

> *"... consider your calling, brothers and sisters, that there were not many wise according to the flesh, not many mighty, not many noble; but God has chosen the foolish things of the world to shame the wise, and God has chosen the weak things of the world to shame the things which are strong, and the insignificant things of the world and the despised God has chosen, the things that are not, so that He may nullify the things that are, so that no human may boast before God"* (1 Corinthians 1:26-29).

When a believer on the Lord Jesus recognises that he or she is unknown by this world, that should register no concern. Being known by this world is totally nothing compared to being known by the God who made it. To be known by God – for him to take note of us with approval – has got absolutely nothing to do with us. The names of great men and women of science, heroic military generals, intrepid explorers and eminent statesmen live on long after them in history. We learn of their deeds in school. Their names are recorded in the annals of this world. But what does that matter if their names are not written in heaven (Luke 10:20)? This world, and everything in it, is destined to be passing away. Tragically, some people literally kill themselves for 15 minutes of fame. But such fame doesn't matter. The same applies for even the case of world-famous names of antiquity that have by their inventions or diplomacy or military careers shaped the course of world history. It all pales into insignificance compared with one thing - and that one thing is being known by God. This was the great truth that Israel, God's Old Testament people, had to learn as taught by Moses:

> *"The Lord did not make you His beloved nor choose you because you were greater in number than any of the peoples, since you were the fewest of all peoples, but because the Lord loved you and kept the oath which He swore to your forefathers, the Lord brought you out by a mighty hand and redeemed you from the house of slavery, from the hand of Pharaoh king of Egypt. Know therefore that the Lord your God, He is God, the faithful God, who keeps His covenant and His faithfulness to a thousand generations for those who love Him and keep His commandments; but He repays those who hate Him to their faces, to eliminate them; He will not hesitate toward him who hates Him, He will repay him to his face. Therefore, you shall keep the commandment, the statutes, and the judgments which I am commanding you today, to do them"* (Deuteronomy 7:7-11).

They were called on to get to know the Lord their God. But that was only a possibility because he'd first known and chosen and loved them. And as Amos was to repeat later: *"Hear this word which the Lord has spoken against you, sons of Israel, against the entire family which He brought up from the land of Egypt: "You only have I known among all the families of the earth"* (Amos 3:1,2). God told Israel *"I have known you."* That was the basis, he reminded them, of all their blessings. They'd come to know him as their

God only because of the fact that he'd chosen to know them. It's exactly the same for Christian believers. The Apostle Paul again says, this time to believers at Rome:

"And we know that God causes all things to work together for good to those who love God, to those who are called according to His purpose. For those whom He foreknew, He also predestined to become conformed to the image of His Son, so that He would be the firstborn among many brothers and sisters; and these whom He predestined, He also called; and these whom He called, He also justified; and these whom He justified, He also glorified. What then shall we say to these things? If God is for us, who is against us? He who did not spare His own Son, but delivered Him over for us all, how will He not also with Him freely give us all things?" (Romans 8:28-32).

We were chosen by him – which is the same thing as being known with approval - from eternity, from long before time began. We often hear talk about the four requirements of a satisfying worldview; we're told it must address the four questions of origins, morality, meaning and destiny. What could possibly compare as a worldview with what we've just read from verse 30? To be known or chosen by God, for the purpose of becoming like his son, Jesus, and all with a glorious destiny in view. Let's break it down: there are four great Bible words that answer closely to the four demands of a worldview. Those words are: chosen, called, justified and glorified. Let's start with the first of them. It all originates with our being known by God (that's being chosen). Then, as regards morality, we're 'called to be saints or holy persons' (1 Corinthians 1:2) –

he chose us that we should be holy (Ephesians 1:4). And what can be more meaningful than to know that we've been declared to be righteous in the eyes of our maker and judge? And four, the destiny in view in all this is the sure hope of glory.

Some have referred to this worldview plan as the 'Golden Chain.' It certainly gives confirmation of our eternal security in Christ. As we've seen, there are four links in this unbreakable chain. Those who are known by or chosen (predestined) by God are those who are called ('the called', 1 Corinthians 1:24); and are again the same as those who are justified; and are also those who will be glorified. The same persons are in view at each stage. It's interesting to note that the final one, glorified, is set in the past tense although it clearly hasn't yet happened. That just goes to show that it's certain to happen, so much so that God treats it as already having taken place. Nothing can prevent it from becoming reality. That eloquently underlines the fact that no-one can fail to complete or fall away from this four-stage journey. We are secure in Christ, from eternity to eternity. Not only is Christ to be glorified in us, but we are glorified in Christ (2 Thessalonians 1:12). That's even more remarkable and is the ultimate display of our sanctification. We will then be as much like Christ as it's possible for created beings to be. We not only know him but we're to become increasingly like him until he is glorified in us and we are glorified in him. But it all comes about because we were first chosen – that is, because we were first known by God.

Everything that happens to us is purposeful if we submit to God's plan. Clearly, it's God's big purpose that we should become like his son, Jesus. That's our destiny: it's to be totally identified with him. All believers in the age to come will be totally like Christ, but God takes great delight in shaping our lives while we're still down here to reflect more and more the character of the one who entered into his own glories by walking the pathway of sufferings.

Coming now to the last verse we read, verse 32, it's worth noticing that the *"all things"* mentioned there are given to exactly those (*"us all"*) for whom Christ was delivered up. This refers back to those already described as predestined, called, justified and glorified. Only those who start off as having been given by the father to the son will receive all things. Again, we see Scripture proclaiming that Christ was delivered up, not for absolutely all, but for all those who were chosen by God. Christ's death was effective for all those for whom it was intended. What comes across here is the God-centred view of our salvation through the Gospel: with the Father choosing; the Spirit calling and justifying (1 Corinthians 6:11); and the Son glorifying (based on his finished work at the cross). This view from eternity to eternity, with the cross central, is surely a most wonderful viewpoint from which to truly know God.

11

A Worthy Distinction

Tennis players who win a record number of Grand Slams, footballers who win many Champions' League medals, or athletes who win a record number of Olympic medals are all feted. We live today with style icons, media presenters, filmstars and so-called 'rock legends' in a much less enduring celebrity culture. Even the notoriously wicked go down in infamy. But, as we've already been thinking, it all pales into insignificance compared with one thing - and that one thing is being known by God.

The Apostle Paul, when writing his second pastoral letter to Timothy, described some in the local Church of God at Ephesus as being known by God. I want to explore with you in what sense he was saying this on that occasion. Before we come directly to that, it's going to be necessary to research a little bit of history – history that's recorded for us in the Bible book of Numbers, chapter 16. It's the account of a rebellion among the ranks of God's people in the Old Testament while Moses was their leader, and while the family of his brother Aaron had been singled out by God to represent the whole people as priests. It was the privilege – not to mention, responsibility – of Aaron and his sons to draw near to God's altar and into the holy place of the tent of Meeting where God lived among his people back then. It turns out that not everyone was content with that arrangement. It began among relatives and among some of those who already had their own appointed sphere of responsibility:

> *"Now Korah the son of Izhar, the son of Kohath, the son of Levi, with Dathan and Abiram, the sons of Eliab, and On the son of Peleth, sons of Reuben, took men, and they stood before Moses, together with some of the sons of Israel, 250 leaders of the congregation chosen in the assembly, men of renown. They assembled together against Moses and Aaron, and said to them, 'You have gone far enough! For all the congregation are holy, every one of them, and the Lord is in their midst; so why do you exalt yourselves above the assembly of the Lord?' When Moses heard this, he fell on his face; and he spoke to Korah and all his group, saying, 'Tomorrow morning the Lord will make known who is His, and who is holy, and will bring that one near to Himself; indeed, the one whom He will choose, He will bring near to Himself.'*
>
> *... So Korah assembled all the congregation against them at the entrance of the tent of meeting. And the glory of the Lord appeared to all the congregation. Then the Lord spoke to Moses and Aaron, saying, 'Separate yourselves from among this congregation, so that I may consume them instantly.' But they fell on their faces and said, 'God,*

the God of the spirits of humanity, when one person sins, will You be angry with the entire congregation?' Then the Lord spoke to Moses, saying, 'Speak to the congregation, saying, "Get away from the areas around the tents of Korah, Dathan, and Abiram."'

Then Moses arose and went to Dathan and Abiram, with the elders of Israel following him, and he spoke to the congregation, saying, 'Get away now from the tents of these wicked men, and do not touch anything that belongs to them, or you will be swept away in all their sin!' So they moved away from the areas around the tents of Korah, Dathan, and Abiram; and Dathan and Abiram came out and stood at the entrances of their tents, along with their wives, their sons, and their little ones. Then Moses said, 'By this you shall know that the Lord has sent me to do all these deeds; for it is not my doing. If these men die the death of all mankind, or if they suffer the fate of all mankind, then the Lord has not sent me. But if the Lord brings about an entirely new thing and the ground opens its mouth and swallows them with everything that is theirs, and they descend alive into Sheol, then you will know that these men have been disrespectful to the Lord.'

And as he finished speaking all these words, the ground that was under them split open; and the earth opened its mouth and swallowed them, their households, and all the people who belonged to Korah with all their possessions. So they and all that belonged to them went down alive to Sheol; and the earth closed over them, and they perished from the midst of the assembly" (Numbers 16:1-35).

Without doubt, that incident was well-known to the Apostle Paul, and the Spirit of God brought it to his mind as he wrote to Timothy who was grappling with pastoral problems in the local church at Ephesus. For Paul said this to him:

> *"Be diligent to present yourself approved to God as a worker who does not need to be ashamed, accurately handling the word of truth. But avoid worldly and empty chatter, for it will lead to further ungodliness, and their talk will spread like gangrene. Among them are Hymenaeus and Philetus, men who have gone astray from the truth, claiming that the resurrection has already taken place; and they are jeopardizing the faith of some. Nevertheless, the firm foundation of God stands, having this seal: 'The Lord knows those who are His;' and, 'Everyone who names the name of the Lord is to keep away from wickedness'"* (2 Timothy 2:15-19).

It's those last two expressions: *"the Lord knows those who are his"* and *"everyone who names the name of the Lord is to keep away from wickedness"* that seem so reminiscent of that much earlier rebellion among whom were found Dathan and Abiram. At Ephesus it was a grouping within the church – of whom we're given just the two names – Hymenaeus and Philetus. Perhaps in part this, too, was a rebellion against the established church order. It was certainly a dogmatic assertion of a strange teaching. What had started out as empty, worldly chatter had escalated into an ungodliness that was eating away at the vitals of the church like a cancer. A surgical intervention was called for. The cancer had to be cut out. The proponents of false, alternative teaching had to be removed from church fellowship.

A house divided cannot stand. Opposing elements need to be isolated.

The summary judgement in this instance was not the ground opening up to swallow the dissenting voices, but separating the church from them and so separating them from the church. Those who gather to the Lord's name must remove themselves or purge themselves out from any wickedness and ungodliness. Ungodliness is wickedness: it's rebelling against God. Action must be swift and decisive. Little wonder then that Paul invoked the imagery of the classic showdown against rebels in Moses' day. Had God not made it so fearfully dramatic so that it would be etched forever in the national consciousness?

But let's visit again the first expression Paul used. Remember, he'd affirmed that *"the Lord knows those who are his."* And here we have the point we're exploring: namely, persons who are known by God. But, we ask, who were they in this context, and what had brought them to God's attention that he might regard them favourably in this way? I think it's safe to assume that this is what's meant here - that God was looking on those so described with approval. For, of course, God in his omniscience knows everything and everyone. Surely then, this is God taking special notice of some. Something like this happened in the final days of the Old Testament, as recorded in the Book of Malachi:

> *"Then those who feared the Lord spoke to one another, and the Lord listened attentively and heard it, and a book of remembrance was written before Him for those who fear the Lord and esteem His name. 'And they will be Mine,'*

says the Lord of armies, 'on the day that I prepare My own possession, and I will have compassion for them just as a man has compassion for his own son who serves him. So you will again distinguish between the righteous and the wicked, between one who serves God and one who does not serve Him'" (Malachi 3:16,17).

During that particular time of decline and apostasy, God was paying attention to those who were God-fearing. Surely, he always does that. It was no different at Ephesus in the first century. God had been noting the faithful brothers in the Church at Ephesus where Timothy was working. They're mentioned in verse 2 where they're described as the reliable men Timothy is to pass on the baton of truth to. Then verse 15 talks about those working with his Word in a way that God approved; they being the accurate Bible teachers there. Later in the chapter he goes on to mention certain men as *"vessels of honour"* and *"the Lord's bondservant."* Is it not safe to conclude that – running down through this chapter - all these are descriptions of those whom the Lord knew as belonging to him, as being his? This didn't include all believers there; specifically it didn't include those, like Hymenaeus and Philetus, who'd gone astray from the truth. Those two were men who seem to have known the truth before going astray from it. Those known by the Lord in this sense are all those whose faithful service is affirmed in their present service for him. Those who are sanctified, useful to the master, prepared for every good work (v.21). Now that's something to aspire towards: to follow Christ faithfully and be affirmed with knowing approval by his father.

12

Responding to Revelation

We're surrounded today with a celebrity culture. Style icons, media presenters, filmstars and rock legends, as they're called, become household names around the world. To be known by billions around the globe is the dream some aspire to, but it all pales into hopeless insignificance compared with one thing - and that one thing is being known by God. The Apostle Paul said: *"If anyone thinks that he knows anything, he has not yet known as he ought to know; but if anyone loves God, he is known by Him"* (1 Corinthians 8:3). A little later in that same letter to the Corinthians, he added: *"For now we see in a mirror dimly, but then face to face; now I know in part, but then I will know fully, just as I also have been fully known"* (1 Corinthians 13:12).

As predicted by the Bible prophet Daniel (12:4) knowledge has increased, and the rate of accumulating knowledge is accelerating, greatly assisted by global communication in what many would recognise as 'the end time.' Human understanding and achievements are impressive. But we may have all knowledge and still it is nothing if we are not known by God so that, in turn, we may know him. Let's hear more along these lines coming from the famous 'hymn of love,' the thirteenth chapter of First Corinthians:

> *"If I ... know all mysteries and all knowledge, ... but do not have love, I am nothing ... love never fails; but if there are gifts of prophecy, they will be done away with; if there are tongues, they will cease; if there is knowledge, it will be done away with. For we know in part and prophesy in part; but when the perfect comes, the partial will be done away with. When I was a child, I used to speak like a child, think like a child, reason like a child; when I became a man, I did away with childish things. For now we see in a mirror dimly, but then face to face; now I know in part, but then I will know fully, just as I also have been fully known"* (1 Corinthians 13:2,8-12).

These verses have been quite controversial among Christians. Paul clearly says prophecies and speaking in tongues and partial knowledge were going to pass away. The hotly debated topic concerns the timing as to when these things would cease. It certainly is capable of being understood as meaning that, first of all, additional prophetic utterances that added to scripture stopped once the whole canon of scripture was completed (was 'perfect'). They were no longer needed or even legitimate once we had the all-sufficient Word, as in the Reformers' cry of 'sola scriptura.' Further, it's also possible to see that the need for speaking in tongues to initially confirm the witness of the first generation to hear the Lord was outgrown, when, as in Paul's imagery of a child's development, the entire movement of the Holy Spirit came to a level of maturity in God's purposes.

73

And lastly, our knowledge of God's things, which even now is partial, will only become full when our Lord returns, and we shall see him and be like him. Then we will know fully, even as we have been fully known. We've seen that we were known by God from long before the creation of the universe when he chose us in Christ. And we've also concluded that in this present opportunity that we have for serving the Lord, those who do so faithfully and well are distinguished above and beyond that by God's knowing approval. But it's in the future when those who have already been gifted with eternal life come to understand more of what it is to be fully known by God.

Well, it's time to review where our studies have led us. We've mainly thought about knowing God before stressing the point, as Paul did to the Galatians, that such knowledge is only possible if we have been known by God. When we first began to think about knowing God, we endorsed Packer's point that knowing God is very different from knowing about God. This is about having first-hand experience of God. Oxford theologian McGrath admits that his own early attempts to know Christ were marked by rational investigations of Jesus' life and times, as well as intellectual struggles with church doctrine. He had been an aggressive atheist, utterly convinced of the godless worldview. Yet in his first term at Oxford University, he came to realize that Christianity was intellectually superior to his earlier atheism. Christianity simply made sense of life in a way that atheism did not. Yet a year or so into his Christian life, all was not well. He says that he tended to think of faith as a set of ideas only. He loved God with all his mind. But what about his heart? And his imagination? McGrath's turning point came about a year and a half after he became a Christian. It was when he read Philippians 3:8 which says: *"I regard everything as a loss because of the surpassing value of knowing Christ Jesus as my Lord."*

God made us in his image. From that early teaching of the Bible, we can learn at least two things pretty well immediately. First, by coming to know God, we come to know ourselves better also, for we were made in the image of God. Second, not only do we have the God-given capacity to understand something of the works of creation, but more importantly we have the capacity for fellowship with the creator himself. It was Einstein who famously remarked that the most incomprehensible thing about the universe is that it's comprehensible - that it is capable of being understood by us. That's because the God who made it made us in his own image.

We've seen how the Bible Book of Ezekiel hammers home the importance of knowing God. God's dealings with Israel, some of them very painful, were to the end that they (and others) should know the LORD - and, as we've reminded ourselves, this was what Paul came to prize more than anything. For him, Christianity was about the vivid experience of knowing the Lord. It had been no different with Moses in the Old Testament.

In chapter 34 of Exodus, we remember Moses meeting with God on a personal level. In closing our study on the theme of knowing God, it may be well worth revisiting that encounter Moses had with God on Mount Sinai. The first thing that happens after Moses climbs the mountain to be alone with God is that he receives a revelation from God. The text in Exodus 34:5-7 tells us that God came down and proclaimed his name to Moses. God revealed himself by announcing his name in terms of listing his qualities. We get to know God's character through an appreciation of what his attributes are. And then we get to understand his attributes better when seen through the lens of his dealings with the human race as documented throughout Bible history.

As we attempt to draw a principle from this, surely it's this - that in the practice of knowing God intimately the first step is to receive God's revelation. We know God by receiving his revelation and that's of first importance in experiencing the practice of his presence in our lives. Of course, receiving God's revelation today is different from the way Moses received it. We no longer need to wait for an audible voice, or any manifest form, because God has given us access to his voice in the Bible which we call 'his Word.' Later, God also revealed his expressed will in his time alone with Moses. We not only know God through his actions and attributes, but we come to know him as we understand more about his will for our lives.

The next thing that happens in this encounter that Moses had with God is that Moses worships God as a response to God's revelation to him. Moses bowed to the ground at once and worshipped (Exodus 34:8-9). Whenever we interpret the meaning of God's revelation in a Bible text that we happen to be studying, that meaning, once understood, always calls for our response in worship, as well as in ongoing application in our lives. In knowing God in practical experience, the dynamic must be our responding to his revelation - if there's to be intimacy. It's good when that response brings about revival. But why have Revivals not always led to Reformation?

Perhaps, because the biblical insistence on renewal hasn't been followed? Sanctification is the putting off of our old self (by mortification - Colossians 3:5) and the putting on of Christ (by renewal, Romans 12:2; 2 Corinthians 4:10-17; Colossians 3:1-10; Ephesians 4:17-24).

In prayer, we direct our human spirit to the Spirit of God and prepare to receive God's revelation, his communication to us through his Word. This means we're reading our Bible with our mind engaged – with it set on the ultimate truth before it, grasping its significance. Thinking it over, we allow its truth to penetrate down into our heart and so to shape our will. This results in us living out the truth with our whole being or soul, and so our behaviour is transformed. Intimacy with God isn't real unless it's life-changing.

It was for the people of faith catalogued in Hebrews chapter 11, and for one of them in particular. Abel built an altar; Noah built an ark; and so on ... but Enoch built a relationship with God (Hebrews 11:5,6). That's not to say the others didn't have this too, of course, but it's the standout thing in Enoch's life. Enoch pleased God because of faith that led him to desire to live in a godly way when others weren't. His focus was on pursuing the rewarding presence of God. It seems a revelation God gave him when his son was born triggered an exceptional response on Enoch's part, leading to a life of intimacy with God ever after.

The few biographical details of Enoch's life in Genesis 5:18-24 are exceptional. First, the frequently repeated words *"and he died"* don't apply to him, but they do to everyone else. Second, the words that do apply to him are: *"he walked with God"* – this is so amazing that it's repeated twice. Enoch's life overlapped substantially with that of the first man Adam, and God removed him from this scene at a time of cultural perversity (when we compare what was happening in the line of Cain; Enoch is the 7th from Adam, as was Lamech; Jude 14,15; Genesis 4:19-24). After three centuries of godly communion, Enoch, seemingly, simply walked one day with God into heaven. His experience of knowing the intimate presence of God in his lifetime here was carried out alongside normal domestic life - during which time he bore sons and daughters – and he also shared with others his insight into God's future judgement on this world. Knowing God is so much more than knowing about God: it's the practice of the fellowship with God that we were created for!

ABOUT THE AUTHOR

Born and educated in Scotland, Brian worked as a government scientist until God called him into full-time Christian ministry on behalf of the Churches of God (www.churchesofgod.in fo). His voice has been heard on Search For Truth radio broadcasts for over 30 years (visit www.searchfortruth.pod bean.com) during which time he has been an itinerant Bible teacher throughout the UK. His evangelical and missionary work outside the UK is primarily in Belgium, The Philippines and South East Central Africa. He is married to Rosemary, with a son and daughter.

MORE BOOKS BY BRIAN JOHNSTON

Brian now has over 70 books in the Search for Truth series, including:

Our God Reigns! The Awesome Sovereignty of God

"We are still masters of our fate. We still are captains of our souls," said Winston Churchill in World War 2, paraphrasing a fragment of a famous poem also admired by Nelson Mandela. Perhaps it's become a cultural meme, but is it in step with the Bible's theme? Can we control our own destiny, or is it all down to chance? Who, or what, is in charge of history?

To be credible, any worldview must answer four questions - about our origins, our morality, our (life's) meaning, and our destiny. When Brian's daily Bible readings took him to Isaiah 37-47, he found the Biblical worldview does just that in an impressive declaration and demonstration of the sovereignty of God. That's what led to the writing of this book, which along the way seeks to answer some important questions that have puzzled people for centuries:

- What does the Bible categorically say about human origins?

- Does God change his mind?
- Why did God order the killing of peoples in the Old Testament?
- Has Israel been left out of God's purposes?
- Why bother praying?
- Was Jesus' crucifixion simply a terrible accident?
- Does God decide who is saved and who isn't?
- What are God's purposes in the end times?
- Does man have free wills?
- Do the sign gifts operate today in God's purposes?

Does Anyone Know Why We're Here? Answers from Ecclesiastes

A Christian apologist, was once speaking to a large college crowd when he was suddenly interrupted. A student stood up and yelled, "Everything is meaningless!" He responded, "You don't believe that." The student yelled back, "Yes, I do!" "No, you don't." "I most certainly do. Who are you to tell me I don't?" "Then repeat your statement for me." "Everything is meaningless!" He then said, "If your statement is meaningful, then everything is not meaningless. On the other hand, if everything is meaningless, then what you have just said is meaningless too. So, in effect, you have said nothing. You can sit down."

The consideration of whether it could be true that everything is meaningless is not a consideration we expect to find arising from within a biblical worldview, where God is accepted as existing and giving meaning and purpose to human existence.

But the curious thing – at least at first sight – is that one entire book in the Bible is devoted to exploring whether or not everything is meaningless. Why should this be the case? Brian gives the answer.

Get Real: Living Every Day as an Authentic Follower of Christ

Do you ever feel like you're just playing at being a Christian? Perhaps you even feel a bit of a fake or even a hypocrite - but you don't know what to change or how to change it. Here is some helpful, practical and scriptural guidance on Bible study, personal and collective prayer, worship, church life and family life, with the goal of us becoming authentic, credible disciples who live with real integrity!

Going the Distance: How to Avoid A Spiritual Knock-Out

The Christian life is a marathon, not a sprint. It's a contest with many rounds, not just one. Comparing Christians to athletes, and personalizing it, the Apostle Paul says: "… I run in such a way, as not without aim; I box in such a way, as not beating the air; but I discipline my body and make it my slave, so that, after I have preached to others, I myself will not be disqualified" (1 Corinthians 9:26-27). The picture of a boxer is especially apt, as experience teaches us that we don't need to go very far in the Christian life before we start taking 'blows' or 'hits.' In another place, Paul talks about being "struck down" (2 Corinthians 4:9). He goes on to make it clear that he was down, but not out. But, sadly, for many today the 'knock-out' rate is high. What are those 'hooks' that leave many sprawling on the canvas? They are the same ones that godly people have been experiencing since Bible times. This book attempts to bring together some of the notable 'sucker punches' that often get thrown at Christians - discouragement, guilt, failure, anxiety, distraction, lust, anger, pride, doubts, greed, divisions and disappointments. It aims to help us to draw on the resource of the Bible's guidance to enable us to keep our guard up.

ABOUT THE PUBLISHER

Hayes Press (www.hayespress.org) is a registered charity in the United Kingdom, whose primary mission is to disseminate the Word of God, mainly through literature. It is one of the largest distributors of gospel tracts and leaflets in the United Kingdom, with over 100 titles and many thousands dispatched annually. In addition to paperbacks and eBooks, Hayes Press also publishes Plus Eagles' Wings, a fun and educational Bible magazine for children, and Golden Bells, a popular daily Bible reading calendar in wall or desk formats.

If you would like to contact Hayes Press, there are a number of ways you can do so:

By mail: c/o The Barn, Flaxlands, Royal Wootton Bassett, Wiltshire, UK SN4 8DY

By phone: 01793 850598

By eMail: info@hayespress.org

via Facebook: www.facebook.com/hayespress.org